The Mind's Eye

By

Perry Alan Pickens

ISBN: 0-75963-258-8

This book is printed on acid free paper.

1stBooks - rev. 03/27/01

Giving Thanks.

There are many who have had an influence on me during the course of my life, and I would like to take this moment to thank them all. I won't remember everyone, but here goes.

I thank The Lord Jesus first. Without Him, nothing's possible. My Parents: Ann and Jack Pickens Jr. My Siblings: Marquita, Craig, Darryl, Stacy, Yvonne, Jackie, and Joyce. My friends: Collin S. Wilson and his wife Sherry. Roger Hester. Dave Pancrazio and the gang at Midland Press Corporation in Davenport, Iowa. All my cousins-just to name a few-Gilbert Gipson, John Tabron and his family, Dee Dee, Stephanie, Christy, Erica, and Keith, Victor, Placelia, Helen, Yolanda, and Victor Jr. Aunts Jo, Lola, Lillie Mae and Neregie. Nephews and Nieces: Jamie, Tasha, Craig Jr., Tony, Adrian, Dominique, Maya, Sasha, Samantha, and Devon-whom I've yet to meet. Courtney, Elijah, and Makala. Then there's my only child Patricia-still love you kid.

I'm certain I've forgotten a bunch of someone's. So I apologize to the rest of the clan.

Rev. Lawrence Manson and all the family folks at Union Baptist Full Gospel Church. Burlington High School. Job Corps in Chadron, Nebraska. Holiday Inn of Iowa City. Mr Shawn

Simmons-Hey, I DID IT! Diane Danielson. John Wirtz. I'm sure the rest of you will forgive me if I've failed to mention you. But I need to mention Mr. David Leibli and his wife-to-be as well!

Then there's all my enemies who pushed me to this point anyway. Even all of you-you know who you are too-had a function in life, and you served it. Thank you very much!!

FOREWORD.

This is my first effort at putting together a book of Poetry. Please be patient with me and I thank you now for purchasing the work.

In my life, there was always someone telling me how much talent I supposedly had. Personally, I don't think of myself as talented. I just like to write.

When I write; I do so for myself and for those around me who will care to listen or read it. It's one way I share myself with the rest of the world and my family and friends. These are people I love. For me, poetry is a release.

Thus; with all that said, please enjoy.

Perry A. Pickens.

For the BHS Class of 1977:

I'm more than an equal now.

CONTENTS.

Unknowns.

By: PAP.

You don't know me,
I don't know you.
In the time of Unknowns,
The days are few.
So here I sit,
With paper and pen.
To tell you. You girl.
I am your friend.
So should you wonder,
If I will be.
A friend that's true,
And true to thee?
By that; I mean,
No perpetration.
Hidden fantasies.
Motivations.
A risky business,
Meeting someone.
In today's time frame,
Under today's sun.

But still the facts,
Remain the same.
I'll be your friend,
Without the game.

A Little Is Better than None.

By: PAP

Part 1

Finally saw the Counselor.
We had a chat.
He told me about myself.
I told him where I'm at.
I talked about my problem.
How it came to be.
I told him many things,
that are, yet ought not be.
He sat and he listened,
to all I had to say.
Then looked me in the eye and,
I got the truth today.
As man enough as possible,
and diplomatic too.
He gave me his opinion,
on what I had to do.
We talked about Mt. Pleasant,
and what they offered there.

I told him that was fine, but,
there's something I must share.
I told him of the fact that,
it's there my Dad's employed.
I know that I'd have trouble,
and too much to avoid.

A Little Is Better Than None.

Part 2.

He seemed to think me lying,
until he checked my file.
I heard astonished voicing,
'You're right', without a smile.
He then asked me about my life,
other topics to be sure.
At times I think I was to him,
a yapper. Not a doer.
He then gave me his idea,
about my state of mind.
I gathered I was slowly,
surely, being left behind.
So I proposed a plan I think,
to him seemed possible.
'It's in Des Moines'. I said,
and he raised not a single quibble.
'I'll check it out and call around,
and see you tomorrow.'
I answered 'See you then,

whatever goes, I will not sorrow'.
Whatever happens, surely will,
and I won't be undone.
For Christ said I can win with Faith.
A little is better than none.

Questions.

By: PAP.

Every day and every hour,
Someone generates the power.
Wanting answers from the sky,
Every minute asking why.
For everything there are the reasons,
And in the year there are four seasons.
Each one different; brand and new,
You ask me how? I know The Who!
A fitting thing; the query of time,
Does the sun really shine?
It crosses the day. A Solar cut.
Run by Energy? Heat? Or What?
Then there's the Sea, and you, and me.
Did The 'Who You Know' make all this be?
Here's my reply: To you my friend,
Within 'The Book' you'll find how and when.
The land we stand on. The stars, and space,
Both of us. Members of The Race.
In 'The Book' our fates are there,
We've got a new home. You'll find out where.

The Night Before.

By: PAP.

She told us to move,
Get our gear outside.
Tonight. The Floor.
Tomorrow. Your Ride.
With uncertain glee,
And some apprehension.
She would not say what,
We hoped she'd mention.
I gathered my things,
Like the other three.
We bunked down on,
Our last night to be.
Another Guard came in,
Told us what he'd do.
Then went for some caffeine,
'I'll be back in a few'.
We speculate. Wondering,
How tomorrow will go.
But in a few hours,
We all will know.

A few last looks,
I’m in a daze.
My last night here,
Before the Next Phase.

Inside Of The Dream.

By: PAP.

She walked into my little space,
oblivious to my startled face.
Ignoring my slowed-down time,
she knew that she was very fine.

Climbing out of her Military Suit,
Then cuddling next to me to boot.
Despite the glitter of her figure,
I knew what she'd intend to trigger.

Not knowing what else there was to do,
Still not believing. Though it was true.
Reacting as I knew I would,
Pleasing her as only I could.

But also realizing that I dream,
The happening's not as it seems.
I open one, then both my eyes,
And see the ceiling that is my sky.

In Transit.

By: PAP.

Night or day,
it's still the same way.
regardless what you do,
it's still around you.
Another year gone by,
the corroborated sky,
sees a young Black son,
turn to forty and one.
Soon The Hawk is here,
Winterized I fear.
When the Robins take flight,
and long is the night.
Fashions will change,
rearranged.
Soft to Heavy,
Durable and Steady.
So you turn down the heat,
I say and repeat.
'Save your energy dude'.
Cease being crude.

And to you Lady,
don't be so hasty.
Turn your Credit Card down,
don't spend like a clown.
I state my case,
before Fall's replaced.
Listen! I said.
Please use your head.
Soon it won't be long,
before you know it? Gone!
It's the way God planned it,
The Season In Transit.

The Appointment.

By: PAP.

Couldn't do it tomorrow,
had to be today.
Can't miss my money,
not on Thursday.
Called my Contact,
told him my needs.
I knew he'd listen,
and hoped he'd heed.
Asked him if the day before,
was asking a bit much.
He said he'd swing it.
"Be there, or bust".
I answered I'd be waiting,
please don't be late.
Said he had to hurry,
to catch another date.
Took my wash and shower,
and did it quick.
Then take care of the business,
had to make things click.

Time to go,
And I took my leave.
"I'll be back roomies",
And if not, don't grieve.
Took my car to the place,
Had to wait around.
I'd been an hour early,
As I had found.
Told the Staff I'd be back,
The lady said: "Wait".
The look in her eye said,
The same power trait.
Now I sit and write this poem,
While my contact reads.
It's the Journal I keep,
Closely he heeds.
Then I'm done and gone,
I'm on my way.
"See you next month,
But not on Thursday".

April's Showers.

By" PAP.

They tell me: April's Showers,
Truly do bring out all of May's Flowers.
To me; you're all of that,
As I caress all of your back.

To hear you laughing delightedly,
While rubbing down your middle back.
I also hear you taunt me with:
"You don't have to ask!"

To run my fingers through your,
Every hair. Top, front, and side.
You know I love to do that.
With you I'll always abide.

Getting intimate with you and,
Enjoying playful fun.
With you, I love the things we do,
All day, under the sun.

Then finally you take and guide me,
With your female essence and power.
You know I can't resist your love,
And more of which with me, you shower!

One Chance.

By: PAP

You're thinking about romance.
I just want one chance.
You've been hurt.
Betrayed.
But all I can ask your for is,
One chance.
I won't tell you how I'll act,
If you commit to me.
I'll just show you.
If you give me,
One chance.
If we are what we eat;
Then I hope I'm a treat to you.
Will you give to me,
One chance?
Now you know where I'm at,
And my heart too.
Here's your one chance again,
Here I am.

Rage and Fear.

By: PAP

I'm Angry,
bitter.
Resentful,
hurting.
Jealous,
Saddened.
Troubled,
miserable.
Woeful,
Full of Wrath.
This is my Rage!
I'm Terrified.
Trembling.
Frightened.
Hesitant.
Remorseful.
Unassertive.
Scared.
Unsure.
Cowardly.

Full of Reluctance.

This is my Fear.

And I own both.

Don't.

By: PAP

Don't worry pretty one,
Because I care.
Don't worry pretty one,
Bacause I'll share.

Don't trip pretty one,
I will support.
Don't trip pretty one,
I will comfort.

Don't cry pretty one,
For you can smile.
Don't cry pretty one,
I'm here for awhile.

Don't fret pretty one,
For we are yet young.
Don't fret pretty one,
Whenever you're done.

Don’t give up pretty one,
For we can make it.
Don’t give up pretty one.
We don’t have to fake it.

Don’t!

What I Feel.

By: PAP

She's gone.
Totally out of my life.
It was never certain,
I suppose, never right.

The same old scenario,
And you know how it goes.
The Black/White Thing,
By now you know.

Yeah. I feel empty.
You could say I'm hurt.
There's no Starship for me,
Like James T. Kirk.

So I sit here alone,
As I write these rhymes.
I'm feeling really old,
As I'm running out of time.

No guessing about it,
The facts are too real.
Nothing left inside,
And that's what I feel.

Expressions.

By: PAP

You think you know,
what I'm about.
Yet you refuse,
to check me out.

You think that I,
might scar your soul.
Oh yes. You fear,
what you don't know.

You believe I just,
might use you up.
I thought that you,
were bad enough.

You pray that I,
won't drive you nuts.
I ask; what happened,
to your trust?

You hope that you are,
secure with me.
I too want that,
and more you see.

You want the best,
That I can give.
It's yours for every,
Day I live.

You need to be,
Assured and safe.
So tell me: Just,
What does it take?

You have within you,
The mode and means.
Oh no! They surely are,
Not pipe-dreams.

You could of course,
Just turn your back.
Say what? You can't,
Be thrown off track?

You now can rest,
You have concessions.
It's you and I,
Our true expressions.

No Changin'.

By: PAP

You say that we've been through a lot.
The happy and sad. The what and not.
I do agree on that my friend.
But me? No changing, and no end.
You know who I am. I know who you are.
We know we're for real. Our friendship goes far.
I rejoice in your victories. Saddened in your losses.
I'm glad that our paths have often had crosses.
And I do not hurt, over your happiness.
Real friendship encourages continued successes.
For he need not worry about you and me.
As long as he's good to you, that will always be.
My positions's the same, just like my 'Id'.
The acceptance I've made is all that I did.
The friendship we have, will only get better.
No matter the who, what, when, how, whenever.
You have your life, and soon I'll have mine.
Still, we are friends. Any season. Any time.
Now the message is over. My rhymin's through.
Now I pray that The Lord will keep both of you.

What you want.

By: PAP

You indicate you want a man.
One who will be within your plan

A guy that will treat you more than right.
One who puts your emotions in flight.

Though

We've just met,
Over the phone.

You at your 'place'.
I in my 'home'.

We have discovered things, about one another.
Things that make me shake and shudder.

Companionship

To put it so blunt.
That is what you need,
And also what you want.

The Experience.

By: PAP

I long to feel you,
Touch you. Have you know.
My love to you,
Will always go.
For what you do,
For me it seems.
Impossible. Only,
In a dream.
Because of you,
I'm joyous. Excited.
With you, I surely,
Must be united.
The days I spend with you,
Are real.
Not cerebral,
And they're the deal.
Our time together,
Means much to me.
It's then and always,
The experience of thee.

Blessings.

By:PAP

The circle of years,
Again this time.
I am blessed,
To be yours.
Though I cannot,
Touch you now.
I am blessed knowing,
You love me.
Fortune smiles on me.
Most men don't know,
What I do.
Ours is a union,
I am beyond grateful for.
When we meet again,
We shall truly soar.
So many times I,
Dwell on what was.
However, since meeting you.
Failure and it's memory,
Is no more.

At night when I lay down,

To slumber.

My soul seeks yours,

In my dreams.

Though I cannot be,

With you now.

I am blessed knowing,

You are in my heart.

An Interaction Thing.

By:PAP

When I leave from here,
I will find a new home.
I know,
I will not be alone.
I will dwell with family,
even my brother.
No other, yet.
Oh I see.
You thought of a lady?
Soon my friend.
First I must open myself.
What was, can no longer be.
I must learn new,
social skills.
Find a job.
Go to school.
Cannot speak silly,
that will never do.

What I do with them?
Depends on me.
I cannot hurt anyone,
Only help.
I must also love myself,
And then I can love another.
I will make mistakes,
And learn from them.
If I do not,
I only harm me.
I will speak truly,
With you.
It wasn't long ago,
When my falsehoods,
Would find me out.
Also, I am no Vulcan.
I am no stone.
I will respect you.

I will treat you,
As you would treat me.
I am a man.
I interact with,
My kind.
Homo Sapiens.
Be true to myself.
Cannot ‘front’.
For anyone else.
Use my intellect,
when I must.
But not for show.

Surrender To You.

By: PAP

She calls to me.
I try to ignore her,
And cannot.
Her sight vexes me.
Hexes me.
I am bewitched by,
Her charm. She,
Knows she has me.
Though it's been awhile since,
We've seen one another,
I am still taken over.
Deliberately. She,
Takes her time.
One piece of clothing falls.
Then the next and,
Then. The End.
I cannot avert my gaze,
From her.
Resistance is useless.
Now she extends a tender foot,

To me.
I am hypnotized.
Psychologically Sodomized.
She mounts. Her essence,
Covers me. She,
Utters a single word.
"Surrender".

The Vision.

By: PAP.

Seeing your face!
I said to myself:'She's real.'
And so, I know.

Your image stayed with me.
All the day long.
In my heart is a song unceasing.
My thoughts continue,
On you.
Though separated by many miles of miles,
Your smile remains.
The Vision is a Being of;
Grace.
Beauty.
Nature.
Function.
I try, but cannot touch it.
Night draws close.
My years, though many,
Have left me.

Many Yesterdays have returned.

Because of your Vision,

I'm young again.

The Journey.

By: PAP.

If space is the final frontier,
Then let us both explore my dear.
For I have been to faraway places,
And I have seen many faces.

In all my explorations I,
Have never known a truer high.
For that which I have come to know,
When we, by mail, met long ago.

We started out just being friends,
And sharing deepest, secret ends.
Risking all to know much more,
Seeking to touch our inner shore.

Therefore I first had made my move,
Because with you, I needed groove.
I had to tell you what I felt,
Keeping it in, no longer helped

And you. Also were drawn to me,
Drawn by a power we cannot see.
You too, began to take some risk,
Because you also, sought some bliss.

Of course, there was much more to know.
You know I told you. Told you so.
thinking I'd waited way too long,
Wondering if you'd forgive my wrong.

But you had done much more than that.
You said to me: 'That's old hat'!
So at that time, I knew for sure,
I'd found someone. Loneliness cured.

Then I told you of my love.
Always thanking God above.
You also, had done the same.
It felt so good. As right as rain.

And as we talked on the phone.
Your voice translated: 'Here is Home.'
The sound of you; Resonant. Sweet.
Your Pictures? Good enough to eat.

So here we are upon this point.
Although I'm still within The Joint.
My course: Forward. Not Astern.
My Journey's with You. That I yearn.

A 20th Century Love.

By: PAP

As the years wind down.
Closing.
I reflect on that,
Which I've come to know.
You.
Invigorating and stimulating,
As the scented herbs of the glade.
While others pursue that which,
They can never possess.
I know my Inner Man,
Has passed the another test.
All my happiness,
Trials, tragedies,
Jubilance, joys.
Because of you, there is within me,
A smiling little boy.
While the rest of the world,
Seeks pleasures so temporary.
So-called happiness in Meth, AIDS, and Death.
Mine is in you.

Together.

In the next Century.

What It Could Be.

By: PAP.

Winter's over.
Spring's sprung.
Time to consider,
What was lost, is now won.
You know what will happen,
As it keeps warming up.
Sometimes you ask:
"Am I Bad Enough?"
That depends on you.
What you want to see.
I can only hope that your,
Plan involves me.
You've seen the photos.
You have visual.
Is your curiosity tweaked?
Do you have the Factual?
Don't be dissapointed,
If I'm not as you thought.
At least I'm for real,
And I can't be bought.

You wonder:'How does he
Come up with these rhymes?'
It's simple my dear,
They come from my own mind.
I don't have to copy,
Anyone else.
For I am straightforward,
Original. Myself.
For now, I'm alone.
My life is dulled. Tame.
We could be together.
For Pickens is my name.

Silent Friend.

By: PAP.

All I hear is the clock,
In the night.
I feel the heaviness,
Nothing. Nothing at all.

I see absolute darkness.
It is my friend.
My companion.
In essence: My Lover.

And you are here.
With me.
Your form is beauty.
Undefined.

Sleeping tenderly,
Undisturbed.
And the silence surrounds you.
Protecting you.

My heart calls.
My mind shouts.
But there's no response.
Only the silence answers.

I Wonder.

By: PAP.

Will you love me?
Will you stand by me?
Will we survive?
Will we overcome?
Will our kids be happy?
Will life be quantiful?
Will you accept my love?
Will you believe ?
Will you know for sure?
Will you? I wonder.

Strings.

By: PAP.

It all begins within a string.
Desires, hopes. Dreams of being.
To reach out and to touch someone.
For correspondence sake, and fun.
And you: Tell me. What do you say?
Would you write back without delay?
Or does it bother you too much?
To ever dare? To try? To trust?
If so. I guess I understand.
Remember. I'm an unknown man.
But if you pull the string too tight,
it just might break, with all your might.
But if you pull until it's taut.
Getting no tighter as it ought not.
Then you and I can now begin,
To overcome. To strive. To win!
You think me philosophical?
Oh no. Not me, and not at all.
I'm content with letter mode.
And be a guy that's not too bold.

Oh yes. It is so plain to see,
That I write to you. Oh friend Lady.
I'd have someone to read my feelings,
Ups and downs. Struggles and dealings.

So now it's time for me to end.
I hope you liked the rhyme my friend.
If you'd like more, they're in my hand.
The name is Pickens. Last name stands.

The Hope Within The Dream.

By: PAP.

The image I hold in my sleep.
Is that of happiness,
With you.
I know I'm dreaming,
But still,
I want you.
I want us.
A son,
And a daughter.
I know. I know,
I'm still dreaming.
Is that too much to ask?

The Things I Know.

By: PAP.

I don't know about,
The political game.
I only know that,
It's too much blame.
I don't know about,
'The Illiad and The Oddesy."
But I know you are you,
And I am me.
I don't know the physics,
Of plasma dynamics.
But with you, I know,
How to be romantic.
I don't know your problems,
Or all you're going through.
But I know I will listen,
If you want me to.
I cannot define just,
What is 'black' and 'white'.
But I do know the difference,
Between wrong and right.

I even don't know,
What the future holds.
But I know that it's there,
We both must, and will go.

Remaking.

By: PAP.

They say things change,
and people do too.
The changes I've made,
are for me. Then for you.
I guess you could say,
that it's all for the better.
If it's worth being with you,
then it's worth it forever.
For I had to begin,
with the way that I think.
I must keep it balanced,
and away from the brink.
Then there's the way,
I express what I feel.
It's no longer a sham,
it is only for real.
And of course, there's the way,
that I act and behave.
I'm grown up enough,
not to rant and to rave.

People make themselves over,
to improve who they are.
Inward, outward,
better by far.
By the way, the clothes,
Do not make the man.
It's within the character,
That make him grand.
I say all of this,
So that you will see,
That I am doing this,
To reaffirm me.
If it sounds to you like,
My words are a fake,
That's okay. I know,
It's not 'Shake & Bake'.
I don't do imitations,
Except for a laugh.
I'll come to you whole,
Not quarter. Not half.
When it comes to devotion,
It means all the time.
Even when the sun does,
And doesn't shine.

To sum it all up,
So you'll know there's no fakin'.
Here I am. Come get me,
I am still Re-Makin'!

A Good Self Look.

By: PAP.

I try to put things,
Into perspective.
Periodically looking at,
My life.
What it was,
What might have been,
Where it is and,
Where it will go.
At times, I'm not,
Sure of myself.
I feel chaotic,
Unsettled.
Confused.
And when I look at,
How I treated others.
Used them.
Abused them.
Hurt and,
Never cared for them.
I often wonder:

Am I capable,
Really able,
To rearrange?
To make a change?
To make it credible?
Some say I can.
Others say maybe.
A few say never,
Ever.
So I looked in the mirror today,
And asked myself:
"What do you see in you?"
And for the first time,
I found I really, truly,
Don't know!!

Current Status.

By: PAP.

It is only me.
No one else.
I know it's true.
I'm by myself.

For I've no need.
To lie to you.
All you've read.
Is nothing new.

But I don't have.
To lose my tact.
I'm just different.
I'm not 'all that'!

Or if you wish.
I'll come around.
For you I also,
Just might clown.

I feel. Just like,
Other men.
Still have feelings,
For you my friend.

Finally. This is,
No hiatus.
I want to renegotiate,
My current status.

OnLineGeekin'.

By: PAP.

They say I won't.
I know I will.
They say I'll never,
have my fill.
You see, it depends on,
one's point of view.
Recycle it if you like,
but it's the same old 'do'.
I get online,
and ask what will be.
And oh; by the way,
how does it concern me?
If I'm not careful,
I could lose it again.
My future decided,
this could be the end.
I like going cyberspacing
To new destinations.
Chit-chatting here and there.
Idle speculation.

For where I go,
that's where I'm at.
And please don't ask me:
"What's up with that?"
In addition: As far as,
what I will do?
That's up to me.
Doesn't concern you.
Some folks already,
are trippin' and reekin'.
While others? Online,
and yes. They're geekin'!
Now I suppose I could also,
do exactly the same.
But that's not my nature,
my thing, or my game.
I am one that is open,
to control and condition.
Only when the advantage,
justifies the volition.
Such that when it's time,
For me to take flight.
Only then will I feel,
That for me, all is right.

But for now I am down,
For the screensaver program.
Looking for whoever.
Always a Madam.
I'll forget about those,
Who would like to puppetize me.
For one day, even they,
Must forget about me.
My mind is my own,
I choose the content.
Next time I'm cyberspacing,
I'll use common sense.
Also, I'd like,
Another chance at a wife.
I tried once,
Didn't work out right.
Now I hear you sayin':
"Man, you MUST be trippin!"
I won't argue with you,
You're just pixel-Illin'!!
I have had my chances,
Had some breaks.
I'm not perfect because,
I too make mistakes.

You better be careful,
Before you start judging.
For one day you too,
May take the wrong cybertrudging.
Take a moment in time,
And consider your state.
Please stay Off-Line,
And don't Geek on your Mate.
For those who are trapped?
Well. Sorry you're tweekin'.
But as for me? There is no,
OnLineGeekin'!

Giving Of Self.

By: PAP.

Just me.
I'm all I have.
I'm all I can give.
For there is no more.

You must understand;
If there were more,
And you would have found it,
You would have been hurt.

You would have found emptiness.
Incompleteness.
You would be unhappy.

What you seek within me, I cannot give you.
I struggle to balance,
That which is, and is not good within.

The Sin,
Which brought me here,
I fear,
Will destroy me.

Unless HE,
That is greater than me,
Is given my all.
My Self.
Just ME.

Soul's Empty.

By: PAP.

That I am lonely,
And have no one.
Is obvious to all,
Depression still,
Accompanies me.
My feelings chaotic,
My thoughts cannot be.
Sadness awash,
Within my being.
Though you may be blind,
Still, you can see this in me.
Despair is evident,
In plain view.
You don't have to search far.
The pain I have,
Hurts too much.
It's made me callous.
Discouragement.
Always at my side.
I am now ready to,

Give up.

A Non-Father. Loser. Twice.

That's who I am.

I have said it.

It's true.

Destined to fail.

I've no more 'best'.

I have a Soul,

And it is empty.

Consider.

By: PAP.

Consider this;
You wonder if,
I'll cause a riff,
Or even trip.
Consider this;
I have no need,
To harbor greed,
Up in my sleeve.
Consider this;
While on vacation,
Your revelation,
Brought speculation.
Consider this;
My holding station,
And approximation,
Is motivation.
Consider this;
You are your own,
Sometimes alone,
And have a home.

Consider this;
For me to change,
And rearrange,
Is logically explained.
Consider this;
You choose for yourself,
Need no one else,
Self sufficient help.
Consider this;
No bull, or hype,
Misery or strife,
Am I in your life?
Consider.

The Concept.

By: PAP.

I fixed your image within my mind.
And then had found it truly sublime.

You wonder just how this is so.
Read on my friend, and soon you'll know.

For starters; you are illustrious.
Your smile? Makes you glorious.

Then second of all, there is your hair.
So full. So fine. So very fair.

Reason number three? No not a trick.
With you I'd love to intermix.

No I'm not done. 'Four' I can't quit.
Because to you, I will submit.

The fifth; and this hypothesis,
We come together? Make history.

I must inform you, in the rhyme game,
The sixth reason says: ‘Check me. I’m tame.’

The seventh forms the additional function.
You and I can be a conjunction.

No I’m not playing. Eighth says I’m for real.
Check my desires. You know the deal.

The Concept’s true. Ninth says it’s a fact.
You need not doubt. I need true tact.

I’ve run out of reasons. Ten says I’m done.
I hope you’ll agree that, our concept is One!

The Mind's Eye.

By: PAP.

Formed a set of pictures,
as I'm sitting here.
After a while; everything,
seems to disappear.
Pictures coalesce,
and becomes a movie.
In it; You and I,
and together we are free.
We spend a day at the Mall,
or the beach, or the park.
Laughing like lovers should,
even into the dark.
Then we have an embrace,
on the hood of the car.
Looking into the night sky,
counting every star.
Then I trace a finger,
all along your cheek.
You begin smiling,
and to me it is sweet.

Of course you return the gesture,
upon my bare chest.
I feel goose bumps,
and they say you're the best.
Next Scene: We're alone,
Music, Wine, Candlelight.
Soft Notes. And everything,
Is more than all right.
I draw you to myself,
Smelling a feminine scent.
Within me, the swelling,
Grows. I know for what it is meant.
Very slowly. Gently,
We lock our lips.
Tongues dance The Dance,
As we bond our hips.
Then you take me. Guide me,
Slowly at first.
Before I know it, we're one.
I must not burst.
The Joy. The Passion,
Of every thrust.
Time itself has fled,
Pleasing you? I must.

As your scream of ecstasy,
Becomes a sated sigh.
I'm back to here and now.
I've left my Mind's Eye.

Giving In.

By: PAP.

There comes a time,
Within the life.
To set things straight.
Having someone to call,
Friend.
Would make more than my day.
The point I'm making,
Is that I'm tired.
Tired.
Of being what I was.
I know that inside of me,
There's a Man,
Wanting change.
Along with that,
It would be nice if,
I were not alone and,
Had someone with me.
I desire to settle,
Have a Wife...again,
Kids too...

..my own for once.
Yes. My dream's no sin,
You win.

Chemically Speaking.

By: PAP.

Chemically speaking; moreover my dear.
Atoms get charged. Some far, some near.
Ions as well, plus and minus side.
I want to analyze, your carbon dioxide.
I also need samples of your love hormones.
Each hypothesis formed at, each erogenous zone.
Body Temp's rising past ninety eight six.
Frozen Water just cannot cool this mix.
Let us come together. Create Internal Combustion.
Our equations and matrixes, will compound the In-fluxion.
Since a compound is formed by two elements together.
We will energize. How and, whenever.
An Alkali and Ketone shares a Hydrogen bond.
Let me plug into you.
Electricity's on.
In Atomic Chemistry? Two types of energy,
One Fission. One Fusion.
One is you, the latter's me.
Acids and Bases? One reacts. One won't.
When it comes to you baby? I always Will. Never Won't.

So. Chemically Speaking: Solid, Liquid, Gas, or Plasma.

I can Bond with you Baby. Here I am coming at Ya!

Trans-World Affliction.

By: PAP.

Though separated by miles of miles,
I long to see you.
To you it is a surprise,
I long to look upon you.
I have no one to behold.
And I am getting old.
The relationships I've had,
Have not worked.
My fault? Some. Half.
So I decided to make a change.
I look to The East,
To end my pain.
Oriental Fate.
Could send me a Mate.
I hope it's not too much to ask.
Would you mind attempting the task?

Mirror Effect.

By: PAP.

I'm not going to run anymore.
There is no need to this time.
For to make the attempt,
Would only deepen my anguish,
Quicken my shame.
I keep remembering:
The Wrongdoing,
The Lying,
The Perpetrating,
The Scheming.
And within myself:
I Feel;
The Guilt,
The Fear,
The Hurt,
The Pain.
I See;
The Faces of those,
I've Wronged.
They're still there in my mind.
From so long ago.

Back in time.

But now. I, must go on.

To begin to Heal, and be Accountable.

To Stand, and finally be,

A MAN!

Would you please help me?

Brutal Honesty.

By: PAP.

It's easy to keep a secret hidden.
Some people do it all the time. Deceitfully smitten.
And I know the type: I've lived with such.
Sometimes doing so was way too much.
Hearing War Stories; sometimes if in fun.
Sometimes was tolerant, if not often done.
But constant lies? Living them each day?
I used to try often. I couldn't. No Way.
I remember the times in the days of my youth.
Each attempt at a 'fib', was transparent. Uncouth.
And despite every warning; and yes, punishment.
Young Hardheaded me, grew in false intent.
In my Teenage Days, Weeks, Months, and Years.
Being truthful was alien. Produced many fears.
For my Parents would say with conviction so dire:
"Tell The Truth always. For God hates Liar!"
But still I persisted, in Fraud and Denial.
As I grew to a Man, The Lie became vital.
Something would happen with every lie told.
Truth always came out, and broke deceit's mold.

Or worse even yet; I would lie too much.
Memory would fail me. Truth again in the clutch.
In every sin where I'd broken the law?
I tried perpetrating before God, judge, and All.
Yet; The LORD had a different plan for me.
"You've gotta do time. For I love Thee."
And so it began: The Breaking Process.
Drug Treatment. The Groups: Soon made me a mess.
Not just once; it had to be twice.
Breaking Continued. It's nothing nice.
One day, I'd found I'd begun to heal.
Again The LORD showed me why I should be real.
More important: In order to love someone,
I must bare my all. Everything I have done.
Now today; I know that the truth might hurt.
But Lies and Deceit? Both are beyond worse.
So when it comes to you. I must come correct.
If I don't. The Spirit will put me in check.
That is why above all, between you and me.
Today is the day I live with Brutal Honesty.

General Specifics.

By: PAP.

We can talk about,
The details of line and plane.
But if you think about it,
The approach is lame.
What we should discuss,
Is the you and the me.
Everything involved from,
The A to the Z.
You might begin by pondering,
The question of...
..the thing that puzzles most folks.
That which is called Love.
From what I understand,
It's a two way thing.
If we do it right,
I'll someday try another Ring.
Uh Oh. I see you getting nervous.
Based on what you just read.
You don't have to run away.
It just something I said.
I'll treat you like a woman.

That is a fact.
I am gentle. Man enough.
To prove my tact.
Tell me your secrets,
Let me see in your mind.
I want to know about you,
All I can find.
Reveal to me your spirit,
And how it flows.
Likewise. Here's mine.
And how it goes.
Then there's the heart,
That you guard so well.
You don't have to risk losing it.
And that I can tell.
In my conclusion,
You're more than terrific.
I want to be with you,
That is the specifics.

Still A Slave.

By: PAP.

Deceived. Lied to.
Lured. Then chained.
Stripped of dignity,
Humanity. My name.

Tortured while kidnaped,
Across the water.
Mind, body, Soul,
Tortured. No Honor.

Promises made:
'One day you'll be free.'
Over four hundred years later,
Still lying to me.

Made me help you take *this* land,
Away from another.
Someone who could be. Should be, my Brother.

New Millennium's here.
Not long after: My grave.
My name might be 'Perry'.
But I'm still a slave.

Quality Love.

By: PAP.

It doesn't demand,
And extravagant price.
But only requires,
The Heart to be right.
It's not puffed up,
Or into vanity.
It only wants,
Honest reality.
It does not need,
A placebo or potion.
It is humanity's most,
Powerful emotion.
It does not seek,
Everything to itself.
It only seeks to please,
To serve,
To help.
It will always endure,
Through the good and the bad.
And will also rejoice,

In the success it can have.
It's form is not cupid,
Not always a Dove.
I seek to obtain it.
A Quality Love.

A Better Way.

By: PAP.

We often wonder why it is,
We're filled with so much hate.
We'll say: 'It's greed and governments.'
Always we will debate.

We'll blame our histories of each,
And every ethnic group of us all.
And yet; we won't be willing to,
At once, bring down our wall.

For us; I offer this method,
For dealing with these things.
A smile to friend and foe each day,
And a happy song to sing.

A trusting gesture without expecting,
Payment in return.
For what you give to others will,
Come back to you. I've learned.

And finally. Thinking carefully,
Of what we say.
Given the chance, it conquers all.
Love is, a better way.

Mr. Fuzz.

By: PAP.

Just a little guy,
About three years old.
Into everything.
And grinning.
My former wife's first grandchild.
Real name's Shane.
Blond. Blue eyed, Fuzzy.
And full of young life.
Having oral staged.
Imitated.
Dancing. Prancing.
At times. Demanding.
Learned to walk.
Now learned to talk.
Toys at his command.
Sometimes takes a stand.
This house. His realm.
He must explore.
Filling his senses as;
Only he must.

For he is growing.
I remember Mr. Fuzz.
And sometimes; I miss him.

You Said.

By: PAP.

It creates and destroys,
And it is in our mouths.
Part of us from conception.
It tastes the world, and all of life.
Yet. With all it can,
And cannot do.
In me and,
In you,
It often hurts.
I'd been led to think,
We were friends,
But in the end,
We are not...anymore.
Were we ever?
So I am wondering,
If,
You will now destroy me,
Based on our real past,
And what you said.

In Spirit.

By: PAP.

Though you cannot reach out to me,
nor I to thee.
I can still tough you, by paper and thought.
Likewise. You can too, touch me.

In this fashion,
at least.
We do connect with one another.
Two Spirits!

So remember:

When you are Sad,
when you are lonely,
when you are Mad,
and think you're the only one,
who cries alone...

Remember:

I too; cry with you.
When I'm Sad.
When I'm Lonely.
When I'm Mad.

And all I can give you for now,

is; My Spirit!

On Every Side.

By: PAP.

Hints and allegations.
My ears are ringing.
Voices cry out:
"It's Him! It's Him!"
Interviews from,
all sorts of agencies.
"Tell us about it." They command.
And then, demand,
a Lie.
For they won't receive the truth.
Stresses and strains.
Inner family turmoil.
Because I hear,
Time and again,
"I don't trust Him!"
No matter what I do,
or say,
no way,
will I sway,
the beliefs of others.

Though One had believed in me out of love,
the others will not.
Sometimes I think:
"Why Try?"
My skin represents evil,
anyway.
And those who perpetuate,
the Hate, press me,
on every side.

The Risk of Revelation.

By: PAP.

I might surprise you from time to time.
But if I do; it's because I want to be thine.
Under no circumstances, will you be uninformed.
So now that you know, you've been forewarned.
For as human beings, we must often take risks.
And we probably will, if we want to find bliss.
If that means revealing, to you my all.
I must face the results, and to stand or fall.
We have often written, trying to reach out.
To see what you, and I are about.
We are learning, confiding, without hesitation.
Now we know. For what we've touched,
through the risk of revelation.

AFTER WORD.

Well there it is. I wanted to give you sixty poems, but I decided-since I can anyway-that fifty two is enough. You have a good idea of who I am now, and the things I've gone through in life.

I don't blame anyone-enemies especially-for being where I am right now with me. I have tried to take stock in my life for what it was, is, and could be in the future. Will I do another set of poems? Well, we will see what the future holds. For only The Good Lord knows what the future will bring-if any comes to us at all.

In the meantime. Take care of yourselves.

Be kind to one another.

Please don't Hate.

Most of all, remember we still live on only one world.

We are still ***ONE*** race of beings...no matter what the knuckleheads in all the Hate Groups say. And as a famous Music Group once said: "That's Just The Way It Is!"

You can figure out who it was.

Here's one more. It's the fifty second.

Riff Griff.

By: PAP.

I'm finished.
This is the end my friend.
Or is it another beginning?
Another shot at living?

Hey! All I said,
was goodbye while eating my sandwich.

For I'm hungry.
Hungry for more:
Knowledge.

Finis.

ABOUT THE AUTHOR

Perry Alan Pickens is a 43 year old black male. He is currently divorced and single. He currently lives with, and provides home care to, his parents: Jack Pickens Jr. and Annie Mae Pickens. A high school graduate of Burlington Community High School of Burlington, Iowa, in the class of 1977, he is also the father of Patricia S. Burton and soon to be a first time grandfather! Born in 1958 on February 19th, he is one of five children with three additional sisters.

His interests are as varied as the scope of his personality. Reading, writing, weight training, chess, and music are only a few of the talents this young man has. If you love poetry, you'll love the works contained in this book. He also writes science fiction as well.

www.ingramcontent.com/pod-product-compliance
Ingram Content Group UK Ltd.
Pitfield, Milton Keynes, MK11 3LW, UK
UKHW040016200726
13854UKWH00001B/229